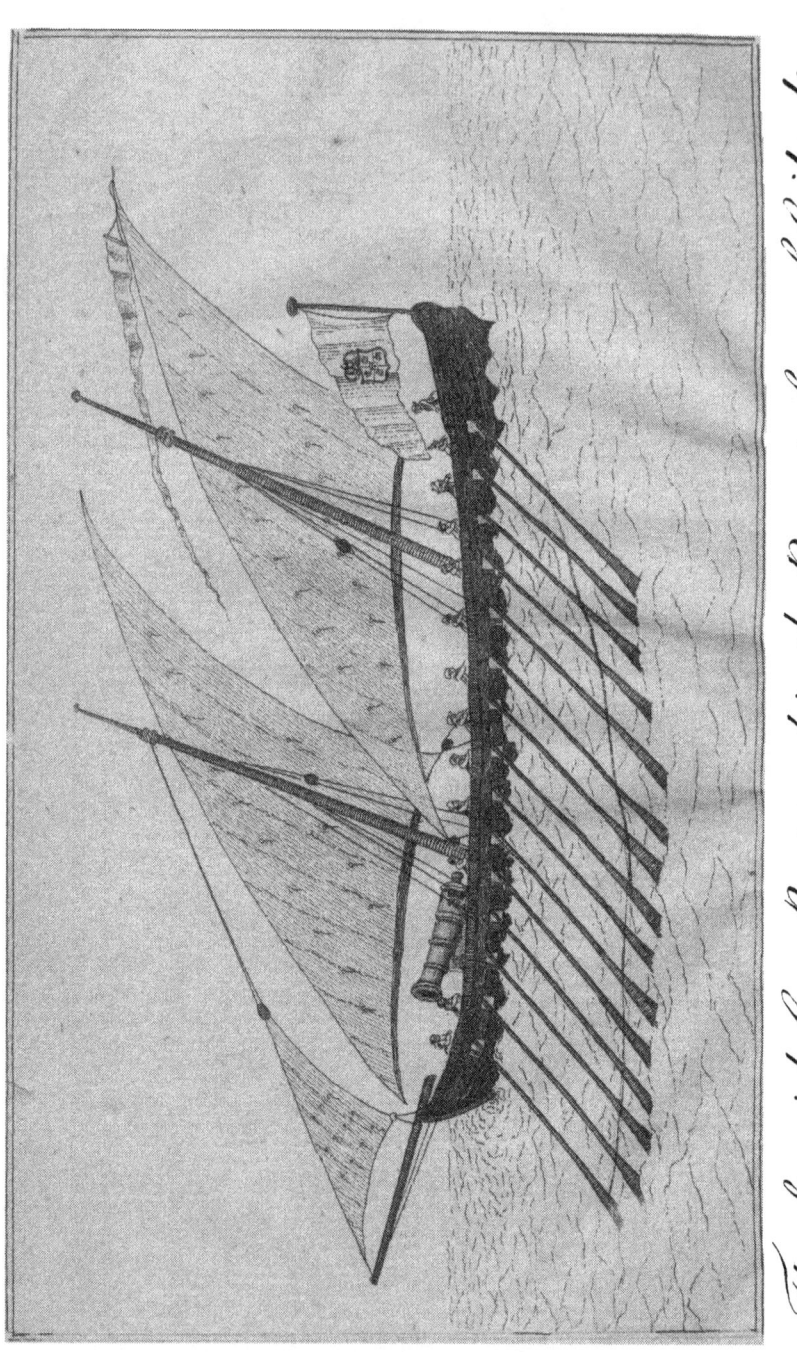

The Spanish Gun Boat used in the Recent Siege of Gibraltar

AN ACCURATE DESCRIPTION OF *GIBRALTAR:*
INTERSPERSED WITH
A PATHETIC ACCOUNT
OF THE
PROGRESS OF THE SIEGE,

The Naval & Military Press Ltd

Reproduced by kind permission of the Central Library,
Royal Military Academy, Sandhurst

Published by
The Naval & Military Press Ltd
Unit 10 Ridgewood Industrial Park,
Uckfield, East Sussex,
TN22 5QE England
Tel: +44 (0) 1825 749494
Fax: +44 (0) 1825 765701
www.naval-military-press.com
www.military-genealogy.com
www.militarymaproom.com

In reprinting in facsimile from the original, any imperfections are inevitably reproduced and the quality may fall short of modern type and cartographic standards.

AN ACCURATE DESCRIPTION OF *GIBRALTAR*:

INTERSPERSED WITH

A PATHETIC ACCOUNT

OF THE

PROGRESS OF THE SIEGE,
From its COMMENCEMENT;

The ACCIDENTS, DISTRESSES, DIFFICULTIES, and all other attendant Circumstances;
The Attempt by Nine Sail of Spanish Fire-Ships;
An Account of the Enemy's burning the Town;
The Misfortunes of Families during these Troubles;

WITH THE

Names of the Commanders and other Officers;
The Regiments, the Batteries, the Number and Size of the Cannon, Mortars, &c.

AND A

Description of their State at different Times;
The Hardships arising for Want of Provisions;
The various Attempts of the Enemy, &c.

TO WHICH IS ADDED,

A clear Demonstration of the great Importance of this valuable Fortress to GREAT BRITAIN.

ANNEXED IS

A DESCRIPTIVE IMPERIAL MAP

OF THE

Rock, Isthmus, the Enemy's Lines, and advanced Works;

ALSO THE

Exact Representation of a Spanish GUN-BOAT.

By a GENTLEMAN,
Just arrived from, and many Years resident in, that Garrison.

LONDON:

Printed for B. CORNWELL, No. 198, Fleet-Street, near Temple-Bar; and sold by RICHARDSON and URQUHART, Royal-Exchange; R. FAULDER, No. 42, New Bond-Street; and by all the Booksellers in Town and Country. Price Two Shillings.

A

DESCRIPTION

OF

GIBRALTAR.

GIBRALTAR, that important garrison, which is now so much the universal topic, and for the conquest of which the Spanish coffers have profusely bled, and every art and stratagem of war have been hitherto in vain employed, is situated on an isthmus, or neck of land, forming a peninsula, which joins it to the continent of Spain. It lies in lat. 36 : 7, north, in the southern extremity of the province of Andalusia. From the north part of the rock to Europa Point southward is generally computed a league. This computation is pretty exact, and may be divided thus: from the end of the Inundation to South-Port Gate is one mile; from the

South Gate to the Naval Hospital one mile; from the Hospital to Europa Point one mile. The space between the Inundation and the South Gate is occupied by the Town, which is situated at the foot of the mountain, and afforded a handsome appearance, the houses having been in general well built of the rock stone, and the streets neatly paved. Many very elegant officers' quarters were likewise interspersed among the houses of the inhabitants; but these, as well as the private property of individuals, have been demolished since the commencement of the siege. This peninsula varies in breadth, and is in some places only half a mile broad, in others three quarters. The height of the rock from the bottom, which on the north side is level with the sea, is 1350 feet.

On the highest pinnacle of this mountain, which fronts the Spanish lines, is built a guard-house, called the Rock-Guard. On occasion of the blockade and the preparations making for an attack by the Spaniards, a battery was erected thereon, and called the Sky Battery. It was amazing to see with what spirit and resolution our British troops dragged the heavy pieces of cannon that are mounted on this battery up the precipice. The Spaniards, who at a distance saw our brave fellows at work, were astonished, and could hardly believe it possible men would attempt so laborious a task, and in the height of summer: they were, however,

however, soon convinced the work was compleatly effected. They perceived an additional fort opened on them, and saw the fatal ball and shell flying from the Sky Battery upon their lines.

This part, and more particularly that towards the center of the rock, on which the Watch-Tower, or Signal-House, is erected, are generally in easterly winds covered with clouds; and it is commonly seen, that while the town of Gibraltar is shaded from the intense heat in summer by the great body of clouds that are attracted by and pass over the rock; the sky to the north and south is perfectly clear and beautiful: so that the people at the Spanish lines suffer much more from the heat of summer, and from the sultry weather of the dog-days, than the inhabitants of Gibraltar do, though but a mile distant from each other, especially as the easterly winds prevail more in this climate in summer than in winter: but those winds blowing generally very hard are particularly disagreeable to the Spaniards at the lines and parts adjacent; as, having nothing but a large plain of sand around them, the whole atmosphere is frequently choaked with it, and large hillocks often appear in parts that were before quite level, the whole isthmus, or space between the town of Gibraltar and the Spanish lines, being a plain of white sand, on which the Spaniards are now carrying on the siege against the place.

The

The breadth of this isthmus near the rock is half a mile; it increases towards the Spanish lines: so that from Fort Phillipet to Fort Barbara, the two forts which form the west and east extremities of the lines, may be three quarters of a mile. A little beyond these lines the isthmus, or projecting neck of land, terminates.

These were the only batteries at the Spanish lines before the blockade took place; since that time the whole line is fortified with batteries of large cannon in front, and mortars of considerable magnitude in beds behind; they likewise advance, by means of a zig-zag work of fascines and sand-bags, to a battery which they managed to compleat within half a mile of the Inundation, notwithstanding a constant heavy fire from the garrison, to impede, if possible, their progress.

The back part of the rock of Gibraltar, which fronts to the eastward, or Mediterranean Sea, is perpendicular, and perfectly inaccessible; so that from this quarter no surprize is ever apprehended: but to prevent desertions by the soldiers of the garrison, who have frequently found means by strong ropes to lower themselves down this precipice, and make off to the Spanish lines, guards are constantly kept, the chief of which are called Middle-Hill Guard, the Rock Guard, Signal-House Guard, &c.

and

and not only to prevent defertion are thofe guards neceffary; but as the fummit of the hill on all fides commands an extenfive profpect, the Governor is hence advifed by fignal if any thing of confequence is approaching from either fide the ftraits, or informed by exprefs if the enemy are making any new manœuvre.

The name of Calpe, given by the ancients to this rock, which was deemed likewife one of Hercules's Pillars, was by the Moors changed into Gibal Tarif, in honour of their General of that name, and hence by the Spaniards was called Gibraltar.

That part of the rock which lies to the northward, and fronts the Spanifh lines, or rather, that part of the lines called Fort Barbara, is towards the eaft nearly perpendicular, and, as before mentioned, three quarters of a mile in height; it decreafes gradually to the weftward, till you come to the Prince's Lines, which is about 50 feet high in fome places, in others only 30; but all projections being fcarped, and blown away by means of mines, it is rendered inacceffible, infomuch that a man accoutred with the arms and neceffary appurtenances of a foldier, and unoppofed by any enemy, would find it a very difficult tafk to afcend this low part of the rock: how then can we be under any apprehenfions that an enemy, with all the weight of

armour,

armour, will be ever able to effect an afcent, particularly when oppofed by an army above with fmall arms and mufketry, and flanked and cannonaded on all fides with artillery?

I am a native of that garrifon, and am well convinced, that, however they may flatter themfelves with the hopes of fuccefs, no enemy will be able to fubdue or make any impreffion on this fortrefs by land; and indeed it is fo exceffively fortified too towards the fea, that very little hope can be reafonably conceived by an enemy of fuccefs even on that fide, infomuch that I am confident the Houfe of Bourbon will never venture to rifk a fleet againft it; for there is no fpot oppofite the walls of this fortrefs, where a fhip of the line can poffibly anchor, and be properly moored for action, but 100 pieces of cannon can be brought to bear upon her, and therefore to avoid the certain lofs of many capital fhips, fhould the Spaniards have attempted its reduction by means of their fleet, they had recourfe to a blocade, to endeavour, by preventing the communication with other ports, all fupplies from entering the port, and to reduce, if poffible, the place by famine: they had recourfe likewife to gun boats, which could never effect any thing of confequence, but ferved indeed to alarm and diftrefs the town's people; they have now fell upon another method, and are preparing floating batteries, but thefe I am of opinion will turn out
like

like the rest of their schemes. In short, I hold any prospect of an attempt to reduce this formidable garrison to favour something of quixotism, and that the Duc de Crillon, flattering his Catholic Majesty with the taking of Gibraltar, may be compared to Cervantes's hero promising Sancho the government of the island.

To return to the rock: All this part northward, from the summit, or pinnacle, called the Sky Battery, to the Prince's Lines, is lined with batteries, filled with cannon, mortars, howitzers, &c. among which the chief are Willis's Batteries. These are the most famous, and do the greatest execution on the enemy. They command the Spanish lines, and can keep a very severe fire on them.

The Prince's Lines have a command over the narrow roads on each side of the canal, which are the only paths by which the town of Gibraltar can be approached on the land side; and, exclusive of the numerous batteries that point on these from the lines, they are defended in front by several batteries on the glacis of Landport, by Cruchets's, and by the Grand Battery. In short, any enemy advancing within the reach of grape-shot would find the mouths of upwards of 400 pieces of heavy artillery open on them; and what army could stand this tremendous fire?

Thus

Thus the Spaniards, well convinced of the amazing strength of this part, always keep at such a distance as to be out of the reach of grape-shot or wall-pieces; so that hitherto only single cannon-balls and bomb-shells have annoyed them. Thus they have been able by this method to sustain our fire, though no doubt with considerable loss.

As no hopes can possibly be held of gaining this fort on the land side but by storm, and for this purpose no doubt a dark night would be made choice of, to prevent any surprise of this sort, a very considerable body of troops mount constant guard at the Prince's Lines, and every guard at the different batteries contiguous have been doubled since the commencement of the blockade: centinels are likewise kept continually posted out all round the garrison at the most convenient distances; a constant cry of " All's well" from those centinels is kept up all night; latterly, at the approach of the gun-boats by night, this term of security was changed at the south part of the garrison, and the cry of " Gun-boats" was adopted, and echoed from one centinel to another. Watch-boats were likewise kept out, about a league from the shore, to give an alarm of the enemy's approach, by the flashing of powder, which was answered by the Fortune sloop firing a gun as a signal to the garrison. By this method the town was apprized.

prized, and had time to prepare for their reception. It was diſtreſſing on thoſe occaſions to ſee the poor inhabitants at Black Town jumping out of their beds, and ſcouting away half naked along the rock, the women affrighted, with only a blanket thrown over ther , claſping their infants, and flying to ſome cavern in the hill for ſhelter, the ſhells and balls from the boats whizzing every where round them, and ſometimes alighting on a houſe, where a whole family were reſiding, as was the caſe with the family of Mr. Moſes Iſrael, a Jew, who was a man greatly eſteemed and reſpected in the place, and aſſociated very much with the Engliſh inhabitants; himſelf, his clerk Benady, and a female relation, one Mrs. Taurel, were all deſtroyed by a bomb-ſhell falling into the houſe.

Gen. Elliott for a long time had ſuffered theſe gun-boats to approach very near the walls, from whence they kept up a pretty ſmart fire on that part of the hill to the ſouthward, at the back of the Pavilions and Naval Hoſpital, where the ſoldiers that were off duty were encamped, and where the inhabitants had, during theſe troubles, erected a large number of wooden ſheds for their ſhelter, with a view of ſecuring themſelves in the time of the blockade from the fire at the land ſide, in caſe a ſiege ſhould take place, not dreaming of being moleſted here by gun-boats. The name of Black Town was applied to this temporary retreat.

The General paid little regard to the fire of those boats, as little or no damage had been yet done by them, and he did not deem it prudent nor worth while to expend the ammunition of the garrison on them; but the mischief done on the nights in which the above family was destroyed, likewise two butchers, one Carrol, an Irishman, and Belilo, a Jew, together with a serjeant of one of the regiments, determined the General to give them a warm reception on their next approach, which he effectually did. Finding those nocturnal visits from the gun-boats now so frequent, and knowing it was done solely with a view to alarm and distress our people, more than with any prospect of reducing the place by such paltry methods, the General came to a resolution to attempt, in like manner, to rouse and harrass their grand camp near the Orange Grove; and for this purpose, whenever their gun-boats made their nightly visits, two double fortified sea mortars, which had been fixed on the Devil's Tongue, or Old Mole, for the occasion, were constantly fired on the Spanish camp, and carried their shells into the very center of it. This camp is about two miles and a half distant from the sail Mole, and in consequence of this, the boats were not so frequent in their visits.

The Moorish Castle, situated on the horth side of the hill, above Cruchett's Batteries, is a very

ancient

ancient fabric, and shelters the town very much from the enemy's fire on the land side: this castle hath stood unshaken for ages; neither the decay of time, nor the battering of artillery, have been able to effect its downfall; but the number of shells and balls that have struck those parts of it that are opposite the Spanish lines, during the siege of 1727, have considerably damaged them.

At the upper end of this castle are two guns, which were famous for doing great hurt to the enemy in the last siege; they are held of no more use now than all the rest of the artillery, with which the whole rock is lined; but at that time there was not a fourth part of the cannon mounted on this part of the hill that there is at present, yet the Spaniards were obliged to raise the siege and retire, after having lain before it six months, and suffering the loss of 10,000 men This great number of cannon, mortars, and howitzers, are all so conveniently placed, and so effectually command the whole isthmus, that was an enemy of 100,000 men drawn up between the Spanish lines and the Inundation, and should a general discharge of our artillery be made on them, there can be no doubt but the whole sand would be strewed with their dead bodies. The enemy, therefore, well acquainted with the formidable works of the garrison, take care to maintain a respectable distance, and carry on on their works under a very ftrong breaftwork of fafcines, fand-bags, &c.

The batteries alfo towards the fea are numerous, and indeed it may be juftly faid, that the whole place is one continued fortification or battery; for wherever a gun can be placed to annoy the enemy, either by land or fea, one is furely found to be fixed: the batteries, however, which on the fea-fide towards the bay are moft confpicuous, projecting out from the Main-Line Wall, are, the New Mole, the Eight-Gun Battery, the South, Grand, and Montague Baftions.

The chief of thefe, and a very formidable one indeed, is the Grand Baftion. This is a moft excellent fortification, and reflects the higheft honour on General Boyd, who projected and infpected the execution of it. The walls are of an immenfe thicknefs, and cafements, or bomb-proofs, fufficient to contain 1000 men, are erected under the large fpace of ground which it enclofes. A bomb-proof is an arched building of an immenfe thicknefs, from 10 to 15 feet, with proportionably ftrong butments, and is capable of refifting the force of any fhell that might happen to fall on it. Thefe therefore are the only fecure places in the time of a fiege within reach of the enemy's fire.

Exclufive

Exclusive of those under the Grand Bastion, there are others at the Picket Yard, Prince's Lines, &c.

St. George's Cave is likewise a safe shelter, and could contain a great number of people. This cave is situate at the south part of the rock, almost opposite the South Pavilions: but it would be a very disagreeable and unhealthy residence, as the water is continually oozing from the rocks around, which occasions it to be constantly damp and unwholesome. It's distance is another great inconvenience, being upwards of half-way up the rock and consequently too far from the walls, or seat of action.

Since the commencement of the present blockade several new caverns have been discovered, perfectly bomb-proof, and capable of containing three or four hundred men each.

The Inundation, which lies without the Land-Port Gate, is about 200 yards in length, and 60 in breadth. It is always kept filled with water, nearly man-height, from sluices made to let in the sea from the bay; chevaux de frize, iron hoops, and many other articles to entangle and obstruct an enemy, are also heaped in this canal.

Land-Port Ditch is a tolerably deep and wide moat, with a pallisading running across the center of it. The north part of the town is environed by this ditch, which has a strong glacis and pallisading in front. The glacis is mined underneath, and a large quantity of gunpowder constantly kept there; so that should an enemy (which can hardly ever be the case) be so fortunate as to escape the fire of the Prince's Lines and all the surrounding batteries, and gain this glacis, these mines would then be sprung, and of course those in or near it must inevitably be blown up. Should any even escape this vast explosion, they would have the ditch before them to pass, and be exposed to a most dreadful fire of artillery and small arms.

The grand battery, on which a vast number of cannon are mounted, is a very strong and well built fortification; the walls are 22 feet thick, and it is impossible for the fire of the enemy to touch any part of it but the very top of the merlins, the main wall being concealed and defended by the before-mentioned glacis. This great battery seems calculated entirely to oppose the enemy only in case of a storm, as the guns do not point to the Spanish lines, nor can be brought to bear on them; but it effectually commands the isthmus as far as the second garden, and would make a dreadful havoc among the Spaniards should they ever venture to approach

approach any nigher than they have already done. The guns on this battery are for this reason always kept charged with round and grape shot, and levelled just man-height from the surface of the isthmus; an artillery guard is also kept at this battery, and a lighted match constantly ready to apply to the cannon in case of necessity.

As it was observed than none of the guns of this great battery could clear round Forbes's, which is at the east part of the Inundation, or scour the Prince's Lines, a new one, very strong and well built, called the Cavalier, was lately erected on a small bastion at the west end of it. This new battery is mounted with very heavy cannon, and would be very destructive to the enemy in case of a storm, as it would effectually flank them, while the former would destroy them in front.

Algeziras, which is a Spanish town opposite Gibraltar, on the other side of the bay, about seven miles over, lies on the sea shore, and is defended by an island, on which are mounted several pieces of heavy artillery.

In the harbour before this town Don Barcelo, and all his little squadron of xebeques, galleys, and bomb-boats anchor; likewise the men of war, that from time to time are sent round from Cadiz to this station, rendezvous at this town. This small fleet,
com-

commanded by Don Barcelo, was here ſtationed to form the blockade, and prevent all ſhips or veſſels from entering Gibraltar; for this purpoſe a part of the ſquadron was conſtantly cruizing in the gut, or ſtreights mouth, to intercept and examine all veſſels that were paſſing to and from the ocean and Mediterranean: any that were deemed ſuſpicious were conducted into Algeziras, and there detained and examined. It was extremely mortifying to the people of the garriſon of Gibraltar, who had been always uſed to ſee a Britiſh fleet riding at anchor in the bay, and commanding the ſtreights, now to behold a petty ſquadron of ſmall Spaniſh veſſels, conſiſting of xebeques, mounting from 20 to 30 guns, a few little galleys and gun-boats ſailing about in the gut or ſtreights, and bringing every veſſel to that was paſſing, to inſpect her papers and cargo, leſt ſhe ſhould have any Engliſh property on board, particularly for the garriſon of Gibraltar.

It was always a maxim with that great ſtateſman, Mr. Pitt, to take time by the forelock, and never to be impoſed on by Gallic evaſions; he was well acquainted, and ſure every Engliſhman ought to be, with the perfidy of the French nation; he knew that no confidence was ever to be placed in the cabinet of Verſailles; they were bound by no honour, nor reſtrained by any treaty; every conſideration was ſet aſide, when an opportunity preſented of injuring Great-Britain: he was always determined

termined therefore to be prepared for them, and the firſt ſtep was to ſtation a fleet at Gibraltar; had that been done at the commencement of the preſent war, D'Eſtaign's ſquadron could never have paſſed the ſtreights from Toulon, or perhaps if they had attempted this paſſage in the night, as was their uſual cuſtom in ſuch caſe, to avoid being ſeen by our fleet, vigilant cruizers as formerly would, no doubt, have been kept to look out, and Monſ. D'Eſtaign, no doubt, would have ſuffered the fate of Monſ. de la Clue in the laſt war when ſtriving to paſs theſe ſtreights, and attacked by Admiral Boſcawen.

It was at the town of Algeziras that the nine fire-ſhips were prepared for burning the ſhipping and naval ſtores at the New Mole ; but this ſcheme, which is ſaid to have been projected by Don Barcelo, and with which the court of Madrid was high pleaſed, and flattered great ſucceſs from, turned out quite the reverſe of their expectations ; for, inſtead of effecting the leaſt damage to the ſtores or ſhipping of Gibraltar, they only ſerved to increaſe our ſmall ſtock of fuel, an article the garriſon was at this time particularly in need of. Soon after Admiral Rodney's fleet had left the bay, after the defeat of Langara, theſe nine fire-ſhips ſailed from Algeziras, under favour of a dark night, with a breeze at north weſt ; they had not approached within a league of our port, when the guard-boats, which were always stationed at a good distance, to keep a look-out at night, gave the alarm of an enemy's approach, by the discharge of musketry. The Spaniards now perceiving they were discovered, and dreading the consequence, though some of their vessels were not half-way over from their own coast, immediately set fire to them, and made off in their boats. The Panther, Capt. Hervey, the Enterprize, Capt. Leslie, the Dutton East-Indiaman, commanded by Capt. Payne, and the Nottingham, Capt. M'Carty, with some other armed vessels, kept up an amazing fire on those flaming castles; the guns from all the batteries in the garrison that could bear on them joined likewise in the discharge. This fire dismasted several of them, and the wind falling, a perfect calm took place before some of them had reached near over, and they burnt harmless to the water's edge; the few others that had arrived pretty near, particularly a very large one, that had been an old 50 gun ship, and which had nigh entered the Mole, as soon as the decrease of the fire permitted, were grappled, and towed off by our sailors. Thus the grand scheme, which was to have destroyed all our naval stores and shipping, concluded only in affording an addition to our stock of fire-wood.

As this plan, however, was well concerted, and must have cost a vast sum in compleating, there is no doubt it was very mortifying to the Dons to see it fail in the execution.

Capt. Brown, of the Fortune sloop, then at anchor off the New Mole, happening this night to be on shore from his vessel, in order to avoid any censure that might arise on account of his absence at such a crisis, and eager to get to his sloop, none of the gates being left open at night, and having no permit to procure the opening of them, nor the letting down any of the draw-bridges, took a desperate leap over the line wall, which is at least 40 feet high from the stony shore below, and swam to his vessel; he received a violent contusion in this amazing jump, which had nigh cost him his life.

When the last fleet arrived from England under Admiral Darby, with supplies for the garrison, the weather being generally very fine in that climate, the gun-boats, which were then only 12 in number, under the command of Don Barcelo, during the time of our fleet's stay, and lying off Rozia Bay, attacked our shipping five mornings out of twelve they remained; these five happening to be calm mornings, not a breath of air on the water, they set out from Algeziras at day-break, and soon rowed over, accompanied by their commander in chief, Barcelo, in his open barge; he ordered the gun-boats to range in a line just out of gun shot
of

of the garrison, but within reach of the fleet, each gun-boat having a twenty-six pounder at her prow, formed a battery of 12 twenty-six pounders; with these they maintained a fire each of those mornings for two hours on our whole grand fleet. If a breeze seemed to be springing up, they instantly tacked about, plied their oars, and made off. These boats could not have dared to venture to approach any of our shipping but in a calm, and then out of point-blank gun shot, as they can elevate their guns much higher than can be done by shipping, therefore their balls can reach farther, but can do very little damage. If they had ventured within point-blank gun shot, the single broad side of one of our 74 gun ships would have sent them all to the bottom; however, the calm continuing for the time above-mentioned, they were enabled to bravado a little, but happily no other mischief was done by them in all these visits but that of wounding one of our ship's masts, which was immediately replaced.

Over the town of Algeziras, on the ascent of the mount behind it, the Spaniards have lately erected a battery, and since the blockade the whole side of the bay, from Cabrita Point to the Spanish lines, is fortified; batteries at small distances from each other are erected all round it; however, these batteries are not sufficiently strong to withstand the attack of a formidable fleet, and I am pretty confident,

fident, were we in a fituation to run the rifk of getting a few men of war damaged, which at this particular time certainly is not a proper plan to be adopted, thefe batteries would foon be deferted and demolifhed. The Spaniards from every part around would retreat up the country, and the prefent inhabitants of Algeziras, who have never experienced a bombardment, would be filled with fuch terror and confternation that the town would be inftantly left defolate, and a prey to the conquerors.

From Gibraltar to Cabrita Point the principal objects on the coaft are the Spanifh lines, the feveral late erected batteries, the camp, and the town ef Algeziras.

The Spanifh camp extends from the mouth of the river Guadaranque up the country in an oblique direction, and occupies about two miles of ground; its diftance from Gibraltar is about two miles and a half.

On the fouth fide of the ftreights, and in view of Gibraltar, is Apes Hill, and the town of Ceuta on the Barbary coaft. This is a very ftrong town, belonging to the King of Spain; it was conquered from the Moors by the Portugueze in 1415, and annexed with the reft of the dominions of the crown of Portugal to the monarchy of Philip II.

of

of Spain, and it has remained ever since in possession of the Spaniards. It might easily be reduced, by an English fleet preventing any supplies arriving to the garrison from the town of Algeziras, as they are obliged to be furnished from thence with all their provisions, water, &c. particularly the latter; sateas and other small vessels are constantly employed in going backward and forward on these and other such like errands, so that this communication cut off must inevitably bring the town to a surrender.

The town of Tetuan in Barbary, lying across the country behind Ceuta, was formerly the port from whence all the fresh supplies were obtained for the garrison of Gibraltar, and for this purpose barks were continually employed going to and fro; sometimes the passage being made in five or six hours; at other times, owing to contrary winds, protracted to three or four days; but as many small vessels were constantly employed in this trade the town was never in want, but kept well supplied with all kinds of provisions, such as oxen, sheep, fowls, eggs, and a vast quantity of Barbary oranges, which are esteemed preferable to any other. Exclusive of these supplies for home consumption, a considerable quantity of goods proper for the Barbary market was exported from Gibraltar to that coast by the Jews, and in return were imported to the garrison from thence large parcels
of

of wax, hides, oil, flour, honey, &c. these were mostly re-shipped for different ports in the Mediterranean. All Christians have been for some years excluded this port, by reason of a foreign sailor shooting by accident a Moorish woman; the news of this disaster being soon conveyed to the Emperor, he swore by Mahomet that no Christian whatever should henceforth reside in that town.

Tangier, a sea-port to the westward, lying in the streights, was, before the blockade took place, the port from whence the garrison of Gibraltar was supplied with fresh stock. This city was formerly in our possession, having been granted by the King of Portugal to King Charles the Second, on his marriage with his sister Catherine, as part of that Princess's dowry. It was retaken by the Moors, who were continually harrassing the troops and inhabitants who dwelt in it, in the same manner as they were of late years from time to time attacking Ceuta. This last town being, as aforesaid, in possession of the Spaniards, and lying directly opposite to Europa Point at Gibraltar, should they ever succeed in their attempts upon our garrison, by possessing these two strong fortresses on each side the streights, they would be able to oblige every vessel, of whatever nation passing through these streights, to pay tribute.

In order the more effectually to blockade Gibraltar, and prevent any supplies of provisions from arriving to the garrison, the Court of Madrid managed to procure a peace with the Moors, contrary to a part of the oath taken by the Kings of Spain at their coronation to maintain a constant war with the infidels. Soon after this peace was obtained, they bargained with the Emperor for a certain sum, and farmed for a term of years all the seaports contiguous to Gibraltar. Thus no British vessel was suffered, during the blockade, to take shelter in, or load provisions from, these ports. Several merchant vessels coming from England for the garrison, at the commencement of the war, with valuable cargoes on board, not apprized of this change, when attacked by the Spanish cruizers on entering the streights, made for Tangier as for a neutral port, but there the Spaniards made prize of them.

It is said the Emperor of Morocco first offered these ports to the English on the same terms granted to the Spaniards. It is certain, whatever outward appearance these people may shew one another, their ancient animosity will in some measure subsist; they cannot easily forget the long and bloody wars kept up between them: and it is likewise well known, that all along the sea coast of Barbary, Algiers, Tunis, &c. the English are
preferred

preferred and esteemed among the Mahometans before all other nations. The blockade, by means of this truce and purchase of the ports, seemed to promise very favourable to the Spaniards; their cruizers were very vigilant at the commencement of this business, and it was deemed almost impossible to pass the streights, even in a strong wind and dark night, with security; a few small boats, notwithstanding, managed in calm weather, by favour of the night, to get over to a port of Barbary, opposite the bay of Gibraltar; they generally carried a packet from the Governor to be forwarded to England, and returned with a few goats, fowls, &c. these were sold at a proportionable price to the risk the proprietors of these boats concluded they had run: the Spaniards, without doubt, would have treated prisoners taken on such errands with uncommon severity. Thus the poor inhabitants, who had no provisions from the King's stores, which, though salt, would at this time have proved very acceptable, were in a worse situation than the private soldiers of the King's army, and were under a necessity of paying a most enormous price for every article in the provision way. The proprietors of the gardens at the Land-Port, when attempting to bring in vegetables, being fired at by the Spaniards from their new-erected Mill Battery, and the fishing-boats belonging to the town annoyed by the Spanish gun-boats, occasioned these articles, though in plenty round the place, to be likewise at an enormous price. From the hazard the gardeners were at to gather their plants, a cabbage was fold at four rials, or 1s. 6d. fterling; a cauliflower 2s. carrots and turnips 11d. fterling per fmall bunch; all other roots in proportion. The price of fifh, which was before in the garrifon immenfely cheap, from the vaft quantity and variety with which the waters around it teem, was now fold at an amazing price; a few bream, that before were fold at 2d. fterling, now brought 2s. 6d. a pair of middling foles 7s. mackarel, from the greater number caught, were the moft moderate; and a ftring of thefe, generally confifting of three fifh, was fold at 1s. before 2d. would have been thought a high price for them. All kinds of meat were at an excefive price; beef, which was only now and then to be had from fome old milch cows being killed that had been reared in the place, was fold at eight rials, or 3s. per lb. veal 4s. fowls 10s. 6d. each, a goofe or turkey at 30s. the moft reafonable frefh meat to be obtained at this time was pork, from pigs bred in the garrifon; this was at 2s. 6d. per pound; butter, cheefe, and loaf fugar, were generally at 2s. and 2s. 6d. per pound; bread at this juncture was alfo exceedingly fcarce, infomuch that the bakers' doors being conftantly crowded by the great multitude wanting it, and not being able to fupply the whole of them, the doors were kept barred, and only a fmall hole permitted, through which the people delivered their money, with cloths or handkerchiefs to receive their bread, or such quota as the baker judged he could spare. As many scuffles ensued among the people on these occasions, every one fighting to obtain the foremost place at the door, the Governor was informed of the great distress of the inhabitants for want of this article, and the trouble and confusion that attended its delivery by the bakers; to prevent this last the General ordered two serjeants of the garrison, armed, to be posted, one on each side of the door, and to preserve good behaviour among the crowd. The General likewise ordered, after being presented with an account of the quantity of flour in each baker's possession, that such a parcel, and no more, should be baked and issued out daily, and limited the quantity to be delivered, in proportion to the family that was to receive it, at the baker's peril to exceed it. Thus the inhabitants, wanting a sufficiency of bread from the bakers, were compelled to pay 1s. per pound for old worm-eaten biscuit; and as even this was scarce, and not always to be met with, they were glad to secure a few pounds of it at this extravagant price, when occasion offered. I find at this juncture flour is at 8l. sterling per barrel, and several other necessary articles in the eatable way at a very high price.

Lord Howe's fleet will, no doubt, be a most happy and pleasing sight to that garrison; and, I dare say, will throw in such a vast supply of every thing

thing useful in the provision and ammunition way as will make them perfectly happy, and prevent the Spaniards from entertaining any longer the vain idea of becoming masters of this most important fortress.

It is proper here to observe, that, notwithstanding this long and strict blockade of Gibraltar, his Majesty's forces there, during the whole time, were never in absolute want of provisions. The King's stores were more exhausted just before Admiral Rodney's arrival than they have ever been since, and even at that time there was a stock of full allowance for the whole garrison for four months. The inhabitants not having those stores to be supplied from, and obliged to pay a most enormous price for every thing they could procure for their support, laboured under the greatest difficulty in this blockade, particularly as the trade of the place was quite cut off, and the means of making money entirely prevented. Fire-wood was an article likewise at this time excessive dear, 3 Drs. 4 Rs. or 10s. 6d. sterling, was the price of 1 Cwt. of wet ship-wood. And here I must take notice, that if Englishmen entertained those ideas of things Spaniards in general do, they would believe, no doubt, that some good Saint had interceeded with the Deity for them at this particular juncture: a storm of wind and rain came on, and held very violent all night; in the morning, to the great joy of the garrison, especially to the poor soldiers' wives and families, the whole shore under the line wall was seen strewed with branches, and even some trunks, of trees, which had been blown away and washed over from the Spanish side of the bay; it is computed not less than 100 tons of wood were received into the garrison on this occasion.

Before Admiral Darby's arrival, though salt provisions were to be had, yet many necessary articles were wanting; and while the whole town was elated, viewing the glorious sight of this great fleet entering the port, the morning delightfully pleasant, and the men of war and merchant vessels, amounting together to near 100 sail, stretched all along the Barbary coast to Apes Hill, afforded a most pleasing prospect, particularly to a garrison so circumstanced. The Spaniards from Tariffe, near Cabrita Point, endeavoured with their heavy cannon to reach our shipping on their entrance; but though they elevated their guns to the highest pitch, our ships, keeping well to the southward, avoided being struck by their shot.

Reports had prevailed in the garrison the evening before, that the Spaniards, who had received intelligence of the approach of our fleet, had prepared their cannon and mortars at the lines to batter and bombard the place. Some who had been on the hill, viewing their operations, declared they had even seen them load and point their artillery, and this proved a fact: but yet such was the infatuation of the town's people in general, not having been used before to see any enemy but who, instead of daring to attack, trembled at the sight of a British navy, that they could never be brought to believe the Spaniards would attempt to attack the garrison in the face of so large and formidable a fleet. Thus had the remembrance of the gallant actions and glorious conquests of last war wrought upon the people of Gibraltar. In their opinions, however, at this time they were most egregiously deceived. The fleet had not all anchored before the most dreadful bombardment took place; bomb-shells and balls were whizzing every where about; the late joy of the inhabitants was in an instant turned to the deepest distress; mothers were seen clasping their tender infants; children running wildly about scared and crying; while the careful male part were busily employed in packing up their most portable and valuable effects to convey them to Black Town, the temporary retreat before-mentioned, situate at the south part of the hill, about 200 yards out of the reach of the enemy's fire from the land side. The bombardment continued so severe and incessant that the inhabitants were compelled to hurry away, and leave the greater part of their personal property in their stores and houses, at the mercy of the troops in garrison.

garrison. They were afterwards enabled, by paying very enormous sums, to procure some of their goods to be brought out from the town to their southward retreat.

The enemy, in order to impede the landing of the stores and provisions brought by the fleet at the New Mole, directed their fire very much to that quarter; their shells however fell short, only one struck the side of the Nottingham East-Indiaman, and the fuse breaking off it fell into the water, not doing the least damage. Thus the stores and provisions were landed in safety.

The Governor, willing to provide against all obstacles in this most essential matter, not knowing how far exactly the enemy's artillery might reach, had caused cranes to be erected at the Rosia, which is a little farther to the southward than this Mole, in order to land the provisions there, if too dangerous at the latter place. In order now to make the greater dispatch both those places were employed, and such was the labour and diligence of the British sailors on this occasion, that the cargoes of 50 vessels were landed in ten or twelve days; the store-houses in town being quite exposed to the enemy's fire, they were under a necessity of erecting wooden sheds at the Rosia Valley and other parts for the reception of this great supply; a great part was likewise lodged in the

Naval

Naval Hospital; there being, however, a want of room to contain the whole, such articles as could not suffer by being exposed to the weather, such as barrels of beef, pork, &c. were left to remain in convenient places unsheltered. In order to annoy the camp at the back of the Naval Hospital and South Pavilion, as well as the Black Town, the Spaniards frequently attempted to reach those parts from their Mill Battery or advanced work at the third garden, but they were never able to effect it; once, indeed, the wind blowing very fresh from the northward, part of a shell, which had burst in the air, fell into the house of a Mr. Maxwell, at Black Town, and made its way through the bed of Major Baugh, of the 39th regiment, who then resided in the said house; the same day one fell between George's Vineyard and the South Pavilion; this distance was about 200 yards farther than any had ever reached before, and was attributed by the artillery people of Gibraltar to the high north wind blowing at that time.

The bombardment which began the 12th of April, 1781, continued very fierce for three months, it then began to lessen a little; in this time the enemy had made considerable havoc among the houses of the inhabitants, but the strong walls of the fortifications were not in the least injured; thus, after the Spaniards had expended upwards of 150,000 balls and 60,000 thirteen-inch

inch shells, the garrison was in as good a state of defence as when the siege first commenced; any little damage done to the walls was instantly repaired: the only injury received by this constant and tremendous fire was, that of dismounting a few pieces of cannon at Willis's battery, which were immediately replaced; a howitzer was also disabled by the fall of a shell; and in the course of the attack about 120 men have been killed, and 250 wounded. In regard to the sufferings of the inhabitants from this fire, it may easily be conceived that those of them who possessed the greatest property and houses in the town were the most considerable sufferers: of these the principal were William Davis, Esq. a Mr. Kelly, Mr. Daniel, Mr. Pearson, Mess. Lynch's, Mess. Hind and Co. Mr. William Boyd, Mr. Henry Cowper, Mr. George Boyd, Mrs. Eliza Terry, Mr. Thomas Field; there were some Jews and Roman inhabitants likewise who possessed property in the place, and must of course have suffered proportionably; of the former Mr. Isaac Aboab, Mr. Abraham and Saul Cohen, Mr. Abudarham, Taurel, and Cansino, were the principal; of the Roman Catholic proprietors Mr. Portugal, Gavino, Delarosa, Porro, Martines, Montobio, Vialle, were the chief; the damage done to the houses of these gentlemen, &c. is computed by the best judges to amount at least to 80,000l. sterling; those houses would not have suffered so much, had not some of the soldiers

diers of the regiments in garrison been induced, in order to erect themselves wooden sheds at the southward of the place, to commit depredations on the timber work.

The sally which General Elliott planned to be made on the Spanish advanced works was a well-concerted scheme, and executed with that spirit and good conduct which, on such occasions, ever distinguishes Englishmen. As those enterprizes are generally undertaken in a particular dark night, in order therefore the more to deceive the enemy, a moon-light night on the 27th of November, 1781, was made choice of; the moon's disappearance being about two o'clock in the morning, by which time every thing being prepared, the troops, ranged under their several conductors, headed by General Ross, marched silently out at the Landport Gate, and formed after passing beyond the Inundation. General Elliott in person accompanied this sally. They had not proceeded far when some out-centinels of the enemy perceived them, and fired: this alarm was luckily, however, misunderstood by the Spanish guard at the Mill Battery, who supposed it to be only some of their own troops deserting to the garrison, and these centinels firing at them. This discovery, however, induced our people to march up with the greatest haste; they soon arrived at the advanced works, flew up to the enemy, and carried them with the loss of only three

men

men killed and eight flightly wounded. The Spaniards fled to the lines, leaving feveral flain behind them on the fands. Our troops were now in poffeffion of this ftrong work, which had coft an immenfe fum to compleat, and had been near two years in erecting. The cannon and mortars found here were immediately fpiked up, and the neceffary combuftibles which had been carried out by the artillery under Capt. Wittam, affifted by the artificer company under Lieutenant Skinner of the engineers, and the feamen under Lieutenant Campbell, were inftantly applied for the purpofe of burning it. A moft dreadful conflagration enfued; fo great indeed that all the north part of the hill of Gibraltar was illuminated with it. This fire continued feveral days, owing to the vaft pile of timber which the works were compofed of, being in fome places near 30 feet thick. Our troops were fo elated with their fuccefs, and in fuch fpirits to proceed to the Spanifh lines, that it was with difficulty the General reftrained them, not holding it prudent to venture any farther, as the army from the Spanifh camp might arrive before any thing of confequence in that part could probably be effected. After being out only an hour and a half from the garrifon, this deftruction of the Mill Battery and all the adjacent advanced works was compleated. On return of our troops to the garrifon, in lieu of laurel, almoft every man was feen with a cabbage or cauliflower, taken from the

Land-

Land-Port Gardens; thefe gardens lying between the Inundation and the Spanifh advanced work, though the property of the garrifon, could never be approached, nor the vegetables gathered from them, the Spaniards, as before-mentioned, always firing at our gardeners when they attempted it. The Spanifh foldiers were fometimes daring enough to enter them, and endeavour to carry off the roots: on thefe occafions they were fired at from our lines. Thus as they had remained entirely un touched on either fide, our foldiers, who had been out at this time on the fally, were determined not to return empty handed; thefe gardens being before them, they were therefore on this occafion pretty well cleared.

In this excurfion Lieutenant Dacres, of the 39th regiment, narrowly efcaped being killed; a Spanifh foldier had levelled, and fired a mufket at him, the fhot barely miffed him: this young hero flew at the Spaniard with his gun and bayonet, and would have inftantly difpatched him; he however fell down and begged his life, which Mr. Dacres immediately very generoufly granted him.

The number of the enemy killed on this occafion is not known; two officers and eleven foldiers were brought in prifoners to the garrifon; one of thefe officers, the Baron Helmfted, being very much wounded, was obliged to fuffer an amputation

putation of his leg, and died. A day or two before the death of this officer, information being sent to the Spaniards of the expected event, it was agreed that the garrison should cause a gun to be fired as a signal whenever it should happen. On this signal, therefore, being given, a boat with a flag of truce arrived within a proper distance from Algeziras, to receive the body, which was immediately conveyed, with all the military funeral pomp becoming his rank and quality, to the New Mole, where the corpse being deposited in one of our barges, to be conveyed to that from Spain, three volleys of small arms were fired over it by the party of troops attending this supposed interment.

During the time of this officer's languishing under the pain of his wound, the Spaniards acquainted with it from the garrison, supposing no fresh provisions were in the place, sent a flag of truce with a few fowls and some fruit for his refreshment: a small part of these being left after the officer's decease, the Governor returned them to the Spaniards, willing to shew them, that the garrison was sufficiently satisfied with their own provisions, and would not retain nor be indebted for any sent by an enemy.

The troops in Gibraltar would have suffered very much during the blockade, for want of wines and
other

other liquors; but the great prices to be obtained induced the merchants and traders of the place to risk several vessels from Leghorn, Minorca, and other parts up the Mediterranean. These were generally so lucky to escape the Spanish cruizers, and arrive safe: their cargoes, consisting of brandy, wine, &c. were instantly bought up, either by the G vernor or the dealers in those articles: thus the troops were supplied, though at a dear rate, which could not indeed be avoided, the wages for the masters and sailors on those hazardous voyages being very great. Insurance was likewise very high; so that though the consumer paid very dear for his liquor, the importer reaped only a reasonable profit.

The commanders of the several regiments that were present in the garrison during this blockade, bombardment, &c. were,

The 12th, commanded by Col. Picton.
    39th, Gen. Boyd, Lieut. Gov.
    56th, Lieut. Col. Craig.
    58th, Col. Cochran.
    72d, Gen. Ross.
    73d, 2d Battal. Lieut. Col. Mackenzie.
  And 3 Hanoverian regiments:
La Motte's, Gen. La Motte.
Hardenberg's, Col. Hugo.
Redden's, Col. Dackenhausen.

The 97th regiment lately arrived there, commanded by Col. Stanton. This gentleman is since dead.

Gen. Elliott, the Governor, is a moſt able commander and excellent officer; he is ever vigilant and attentive to the great charge with which he is entruſted, the care of this important fortreſs; he riſes at the dawn of day, and immediately rides round all the walls, takes notice of the ſeveral guards, and obſerves whether that due order is preſerved throughout ſo eſſential to the ſecurity of the place. He is remarkably active for his age, and very temperate in his manner of living: in this particular he is a little ſingular, never eating meats of any kind, nor drinking wines or ſtrong liquors; fiſh, puddings, vegetables, &c. conſtitute his diet, his beverage water.

General Boyd, the Lieutenant-Governor, is a brave and vigilant officer, equally diligent with the Governor; he has remained in a ſmall caſement at his quarters in town ever ſince the bombardment; his deſire to preſerve good order, and prevent, as much as poſſible, his ſoldiers at this time of confuſion and diſtreſs from making too free with the effects of the inhabitants, deſerves the higheſt praiſe; and his generous efforts for this purpoſe will, I doubt not, be ever remembered by that

grateful

grateful people with the due fenfe of gratituue fuch a fyftem of conduct infpires.

General Green, the chief engineer, is a moft fkilful officer in his profeffion, univerfally beloved and refpected by the people of the place.

General La Motte, commander of the Hanoverian brigade, will ever be admired for that good order and difcipline which has been always preferved among the troops under his command.

Colonel Hugo, who fignalized himfelf very much in the fally made from the garrifon on the Spanifh advanced work, is a very brave officer, and poffeffes every other virtue that adorns the man in fhort, the commanders, and whole corps of Hanoverian troops, have deported themfelves during this long and troublefome time in fo very noble and exemplary a manner that too much praife cannot poffibly be given them.

Colonel Picton, Commander of the 12th regiment, fhewed himfelf on this occafion a very valiant and humane officer; he exerted his moft ftrenuous efforts to maintain good order and behaviour in his regiment, and to impede, if poffible, any depredations being committed by them on the effects of the diftreffed inhabitants.

The

The commanders of all the regiments in this garrison are men of great military talents, and the inferior officers are excited by a noble emulation to imitate them; an army, therefore, such as Gibraltar at present affords, for the compleat and well-disciplined soldier, can hardly be equalled among all the rest of his Majesty's forces.

There are mounted on the several ramparts round this garrison upwards of 700 pieces of cannon, most of which are eighteen, twenty-four, and thirty-two pounders; besides these a vast number of thirteen-inch mortars and howitzers, 8000 troops with small arms, wall-pieces, &c.

Among the great number of armed vessels belonging to the King and those of private adventurers, which during the long blockade were fortunate enough to push singly through the Spanish cruizers, and arrive safe to the garrison, none gave greater pleasure to the people of the place than the Folkstone cutter, commanded by Captain Fagg. This spirited hero managed his vessel so skilfully, and displayed such undaunted resolution in his efforts to gain the port, that though the whole Spanish squadron, consisting of a ship of the line of 74 guns, one of 50 guns, a frigate, and upwards of 20 sail of xebeques, galleys, &c. sailed from Algeziras immediately on his appearance in the streights to intercept his entrance, he notwithstanding nobly

G effected

effected it. On appearance of the first xebeque which was a capital one of 32 guns, he brought up instantly to engage her; presently he perceived another, and soon after the whole fleet. Favoured by a fine breeze, he now stood away for the Barbary shore, determined, if possible, to get to windward of them all. In order the better to prevent his escape, and impede his gaining the port, the Spaniards separated their fleet in several divisions; the whole garrison were on the walls viewing Captain Fagg's behaviour; in short, he managed and manœuvred so cleverly, that, as he designed, he brought them all one after another to leeward of him. He now stood up for the New Mole, while the Spaniards were all drove behind the rock, Don Barcelo's own ship of 74 guns excepted. He had remained off Cabrita Point, determined, that if the cutter should have been so lucky to escape the great number of cruizers dispatched to cut her off, that at all events he would be able to effect it by running his ship from said Point towards the New Mole. Capt. Fagg, like a true British hero, though he saw this great ship bearing down upon him, and prepared to fire her broadside, which must inevitably have sunk him, never flinched, but boldly pushed up for the Mole. Barcelo, at this time very near fired as he expected; every ball luckily missed, and Fagg, now to windward, and out of all danger, fired his small stern chaces at the Spanish Commodore, and entered the New Mole of Gibraltar,

amidst

amidft the acclamations of the whole garrifon, who were the joyful fpectators of his moft intrepid conduct. The Governor and principal people of the garrifon invited him to dine, and gave him every mark of their approbation, and fenfe of his gallant behaviour.

An odd circumftance attended an Irifh veffel's getting into Gibraltar in this interval of the blockade: fhe had been lucky enough to get well up the ftreights before fhe was difcovered by the Spanifh cruizers; arriving off Europa Point, fhe was hailed, and defired to make for the Mole; the Irifh Captain underftood it was for the Old Mole, the ufual place where merchant veffels lie off in peaceable times to difcharge their cargoes; but, being quite within the fire of the Spanifh batteries, is never made ufe of during a war with Spain. He foon arrived at this old anchoring place, and was inftantly faluted with a heavy fire from the enemy's line. Surprized at this unexpected reception, he knew not how to act. He ftood in for the Pallifades near Water-Port, and was foon aground. Commodore Curtis, feeing his error, went off to him, and remonftrating on his behaviour, telling him it was the New and not the Old Mole was ufed in war time—Arrah, fays he, they told me the Mole, and we heard in Corke, before I failed, that General Elliott had fallied out, and fpiked up all the Spanifh guns. After entering the man of
war's

war's boat, and leaving the veffel, the Spaniards ftill firing very fmartly, By Jafus, fays he, Commodore, we muft go back again; I forgot to feed the few fowls I have on board. Faith, fays the Commodore, the fowls may keep Lent then; I'll not expofe my people's lives under fuch a fire to fave your few fowls.

Such was the confternation and general depreffion that took place in the Spanifh camp and parts adjacent on Admiral Rodney's defeat of Langara, and conducting his fhip the Phœnix, with the other men of war captured on that occafion, into Gibraltar, that it was a current opinion among the people of the place if the Britifh fleet had then gone over to Algeziras, and the Spanifh camp, both would have been inftantly deferted; Don Barcelo's fhip of 74 guns, and other veffels lying in the port, would have been taken, and the vaft quantity of ftores in the camp been in our poffeffion; though I have not the leaft doubt but fuch an enterprize at that juncture of defpondency would have had the defired fuccefs, the then ftate of the Britifh navy, and that of its combined enemies, rendered an undertaking of that fort in fuch circumftances very improper, it was therefore very wifely avoided.

During the bombardment of Gibraltar many very remarkable efcapes were experienced by different

ferent people; a bomb-shell fell so near a serjeant of the garrison that the fuse set fire to his coat; happening to be running at the time, he continued his career with his cloaths in an entire blaze; when out of danger from the bursting of the shell he stripped, and escaped perfectly unhurt. A piece of a bomb-shell, which had burst very near Mr. Matthew Cowper while reading a book, knocked the book out of his hand, and did him not the least injury. An old Black, or Negro, called Maro, who had been many years resident in the garrison, happening to be present in the same shed wherein the two butchers before-mentioned were killed, the officers of the garrison, who used frequently to joke with him, enquired how he managed to escape so well; oh! replied the Black, laughing, " De ball nor de bomb no hurt me, I " bomb proof."

In many of the attacks of the gun-boats they were frequently deceived in the direction of their fire: this deception was highly enjoyed by the garrison; their shells often set fire to the bushes on the hill, which in the night they mistook for the wooden sheds of Black Town, and, as is customary on such occasions, kept up a very brisk fire on that part, to prevent, as they imagined, our people from extinguishing it; but it was the bushes alone that suffered at these times, from the

great

great expence of ammunition, and the heroic attacks of the gun-boats.

The very great importance of this valuable garrison to Great-Britain results from its most advantageous situation, which must ever render it, what Mr. Pitt termed it in one of his speeches, the most inestimable jewel in the British crown.

The streights where it is situated, and to which it gives name, separate the ocean from the Mediterranean; these streights being so very narrow, a British squadron, stationed at Gibraltar, must ever distress the enemy's trade in time of war more than in any other part whatever. This alone is a great consideration, as a very capital and lucrative trade is constantly carried on from the French port of Marseilles in the Mediterranean to the West-Indies, and vice versa: it is from this trade being entirely free and uninterrupted during the present war, by our not having as formerly a fleet stationed at Gibraltar to intercept its passing the streights, that the French are enabled to supply their extraordinary exigencies, and carry on the war. Had a British fleet been stationed to guard the streights, this grand sinew of their support would have been cut off, and instead of convoys of 100 sail of large merchant ships, with valuable cargoes, passing in a vaunting manner through the streights, single ships only would have dared to attempt this passage,

sage, and in dark nights: even these could hardly escape, but must fall into the hands of our cruizers. A great part of France, as well as Spain, lying up the Mediterranean, the coasting trade that must pass these streights is likewise very considerable: this would also be entirely intercepted and prevented. Hence it is evident, that the trade of France and Spain must suffer in the highest degree from a British squadron stationed at Gibraltar. The great naval ports of Toulon and Carthagena, belonging to the French and Spaniards, lying in the Mediterranean, their men of war, when desirous of a junction with those at Brest or Cadiz, must pass these streights, where, if a British squadron was stationed, they must fight their way, and in all probability be captured as usual.

The bay of Gibraltar is a very safe and commodious one; a fine port for the trading ships coming from the Mediterranean; they can beat to windward as far as this bay, but no farther. This impediment arises from the current running so forcibly in these narrow streights. What a pleasure and happiness to English masters of ships then, after long passages, that being detained at the streights of Gibraltar, they have a British port to anchor in till the wind favours; and in these cases, as it generally happens, being in want of provisions and water, they are here supplied with every necessary refreshment.

These

These considerations; and the vast sums that have been expended to render this place in a manner impregnable, will, it is hoped, for ever have due weight with the Ministry of this country. By their great efforts to supply it 'tis evident they are perfectly sensible of its vast importance. May their endeavours be crowned with success, and may we see an English fleet stationed and riding triumphant in the Bay of Gibraltar, as was the case in former wars; there commanding the streights, permitting those only to pass whose friendship or alliance entitle them to such indulgence.

Exclusive of those great benefits that arise from it's situation, this place is, besides, a great resort for merchants, many of whom carry on a very extensive trade, and import vast quantities of goods from the Mother Country, this trade not being confined to the town of Gibraltar, but extended to all parts of Spain, the coast of Barbary, &c.

Here it is proper to observe, that did not the motives of preserving good harmony and friendly intercourse with the neighbours of the garrison, the Spaniards, operate more powerfully in the generous breast of Englishmen than all the advantages to be reaped from a lucrative trade, an amazing quantity of Manchester and other prohibited goods might be constantly introduced into Spain through this

this channel; but, as well on account of giving no umbrage to his Catholic Majesty, by contributing in any wise to prejudice his revenues, as because the military and other gentry of the garrison would wish to enjoy the benefit of an open communication with the country, all clandestine trade is carefully avoided and guarded against. The people of Gibraltar are by these means in constant friendship with the Spaniards, who supply them daily with all kinds of wild fowl, hares, rabbits, pigs, and fruit of all sorts in great abundance. Large parties of Spanish gentry are continually coming into the garrison from the country, and making purchases of different articles they are in need of. On the other hand, numbers of officers and other gentlemen are constantly going out from the garrison to shoot, and pass their time away in the country, or at the neighbouring towns of St. Roche and Algeziras. These are by a late regulation obliged to return to town before sun-set, none are permitted to lie without the walls of the fortress. If a gentleman is desirous of visiting Madrid, Cadiz, or any other place, leave can always be obtained from the Governor by a special permit; thus in peaceable times the people of Spain and Gibraltar live in the most perfect harmony and friendship with each other; and no doubt the whole country near the garrison regret this interruption of their former happiness equally with the people of Gibraltar.

The value of goods imported from England annually by the merchants of the garrison is computed to amount to 200,000l.

Annexed is a list of the present grand naval force, which sailed from Portsmouth the 11th of September, under Lord Howe, to convoy the necessary supplies for this important garrison.

	Guns.	
Victory	100	Admiral Lord Howe.
		Capt. Gower.
		Capt. Duncan.
Britannia	100	Admiral Barrington.
		Capt. Hill.
Queen	98	Admiral Hood.
		Capt. Domet.
Atlas	98	Vandeput.
Princess Royal	98	Falconer.
Ocean	90	Admiral Milbank.
		Capt. Roger.
Blenheim	90	Duncan.
Union	90	Dalrymple.
Princess Amelia	84	Admiral Sir R. Hughes.
		Capt. Reynolds.
Cambridge	84	Stewart.
Royal William	84	Allen.
Foudroyant	80	Jarvis.
Alexander	74	Lord Longford

Bellona

Bellona	74	Onslow.
Berwick	74	Phipps.
Dublin	74	Dixon.
Edgar	74	Commodore Hotham. Capt. Cayley.
Egmont	74	Ferguson.
Fortitude	74	Keppel.
Ganges	74	Fielding.
Goliah	74	Parker.
Suffolk	74	Horne.
Vengeance	74	Bantry.
Asia	64	Blyth.
Bienfaisant	64	Howarth.
Crown	64	Reeves.
Polyphemus	64	Finch.
Ruby	64	Collins.
Raisonable	64	Lord Harvey
Sampson	64	Harvey.
Vigilant	64	Douglas.
Buffalo	60	Holloway.
Panther	60	Sidmonton.
Bristol	50	Burney.

FRIGATES.

Minerva	38	Pakenham.
Latona	34	Conway.
Monsieur	36	Finch.
Andromache	32	Byron.

Recovery

Recovery	32	Bertie.
Dian	32	Calder
Proserpine	28	Taylor.
Termagant	18	Sterling.

FIRE-SHIPS.

Pluto,   Spitfire   Tysiphone.

FINIS.

www.ingramcontent.com/pod-product-compliance
Lightning Source LLC
Chambersburg PA
CBHW051717040426
42446CB00008B/926